YOUR KNOWLEDGE HAS VALUE

Anna Fuchs

The Northern Ireland Conflict - How the State to Nation Imbalance Caused a Centuries' Conflict

GRIN Verlag

Bibliografische Information der Deutschen Nationalbibliothek:

Die Deutsche Bibliothek verzeichnet diese Publikation in der Deutschen National-
bibliografie; detaillierte bibliografische Daten sind im Internet über http://dnb.d-
nb.de/ abrufbar.

Imprint:

Copyright © 2011 GRIN Verlag GmbH
Druck und Bindung: Books on Demand GmbH, Norderstedt Germany
ISBN: 978-3-656-40219-0

This book at GRIN:

http://www.grin.com/en/e-book/211619/the-northern-ireland-conflict-how-the-
state-to-nation-imbalance-caused

GRIN - Your knowledge has value

Der GRIN Verlag publiziert seit 1998 wissenschaftliche Arbeiten von Studenten, Hochschullehrern und anderen Akademikern als eBook und gedrucktes Buch. Die Verlagswebsite www.grin.com ist die ideale Plattform zur Veröffentlichung von Hausarbeiten, Abschlussarbeiten, wissenschaftlichen Aufsätzen, Dissertationen und Fachbüchern.

Visit us on the internet:

http://www.grin.com/

http://www.facebook.com/grincom

http://www.twitter.com/grin_com

International School

Haifa University

Fall Semester 2010

Honors Seminar in Peace and Conflict Studies: Regional Conflict

The Northern Ireland Conflict

How the State to Nation Imbalance
caused a centuries' conflict

handed in by:

Anna Fuchs

January 18, 2011

Contents

1.   Introduction

"We have just enough religion to make us hate, but not enough to make us love, one another." (Jonathan Swift, *Thoughts on Various Subjects*, 1727)

Since Ireland's occupation by England, it has been a conflict between two identity groups: Catholics and Protestants. Protestants are usually loyal to Great Britain and want Northern Ireland to remain part of it. They are therefore called loyalists or unionists. Catholics on the other hand are usually loyal to the Republic of Ireland and strive for a reunification of both Irish states. They are therefore called nationalists or republicans. Hence, those two identity groups don't see themselves as one nation but rather as two, forced to live in the same state. As Marc Mulholland points out in the preface of his book about the history of the conflict,

> "Northern Ireland's tragedy is that its people have not been able to agree upon a common identity. Rather than stand by each other, they compete. Being so alike – in language, appearance, and broad culture – they cling tenaciously to that which marks them out." (Mulholland 2002: v)

In my opinion, this is a very good description of the whole history of the Northern Ireland conflict. Throughout history, it has always been Protestants against Catholics and vice versa, with some more and some less violent phases. Although the clashes appeared between those two religious groups, it is important to notice that this conflict is no longer about religion, but about politics. It is about the future of the Northern Irish state, whether it will remain part of the United Kingdom (UK) or whether it will become part of the Republic of Ireland. The majority of Protestants support the first option whereas the majority of Catholics support the latter. But that is only a coincidence, they are competing nations and not competing religions, since neither side denies the other's religion's right to exist: "Religious categories have remained important, but currently their function is not so much to underline religion itself, but rather loyalty to a specific group" (Kuusisto-Arponen 2001: 121).

In this paper, I use the State to Nation Balance approach to explain the Northern Irish conflict. I argue that this conflict perfectly illustrates how State to Nation Imbalance and especially contradicting identities and interests can cause a conflict, especially if the state is too weak to control the different forces within its territory.

2. History of the Northern Ireland Conflict

The problems in Ireland started in the 16th century, when England conquered the island. The predominant religion at that time was Catholicism, the Irish people practising what is called Gaelic pastoralism, a nomadic lifestyle. England then began to settle English and Scottish 'undertakers' in Ireland, especially in the Ulster region in the North. Those settlers had to guard against native resistance and to build a society based on English law, Protestantism and settled agriculture. One century later, conflicts between Protestant and Catholic farmers started when the Catholic King James II was defeated by the Protestant William the Orange, and Protestants in Ulster started denying the Catholic population political and social rights. In the following decades, paramilitary forces were created on both sides and this time was characterised by riots and severe clashes between Protestants and Catholics.

In 1919, a new parliament was created for the Irish Republic, which gained independence from the UK in 1922. The Government of Ireland Act of 1920 declared six of the nine counties of the Ulster region to be separated from the Republic. The state of Northern Ireland hence was created and given its own parliament under the control of the UK (cf. Mulholland 2002: 3-28). According to Scott A. Bollens, the creation of the border between Northern Ireland and the Republic of Ireland led to a "double minority syndrome": Protestants are a minority on the whole island that is threatened by a possible reunification, while the Catholic minority in Northern Ireland is threatened by Protestant and external British rule (Ibid. 2000: 190).

After the partition of Ireland, the so called Anglo-Irish war started in which the Catholic population of Northern Ireland suffered extremely under loyalist paramilitary violence:

> "Catholics were battered into submission. More people died in Belfast during three months of violence in 1922 than in the whole two years following the formation of the state. A substantial majority of the 232 victims were Catholic, and 11,000 were made jobless and 23,000 homeless. Over 4,300 Catholic-owned shops and businesses were burned, looted, or wrecked." (Ibid. 2002: 31)

After their 'defeat', Catholics were extremely discriminated by Protestants; they argued that the Catholics' loyalty to Northern Ireland could never be real and only temporary (Ibid.: 46).

The so called 'Troubles' started in 1969 when the civil rights movement emerged, demanding equal rights for Catholics and Protestants, and the bombings by republican paramilitary forces began. The time of the 'Troubles', which continued until the ceasefire in 1994, was characterised by extreme violence against civilians committed by paramilitary forces on both sides, but also by extreme state violence. In total, 3,000 people were killed by loyalist and republican paramilitary forces during the 'Troubles', 350 deaths were caused by agents of the state (Aoláin, 2000: 13). In 1994, the IRA and the loyalist paramilitaries declared a ceasefire and on April 10 in 1998 the Good Friday Agreement was signed, which established a power sharing government with a veto option for both communities, several sub-committees to oversee executive functions, and a North-South Ministerial Council for consultation and cooperation. In the following referendum, 71.1 per cent voted in favour of it in Northern Ireland, as well as 95 per cent in the Republic of Ireland (cf. Mulholland 2002: 177f).

3.   The State to Nation Balance Approach

The State to Nation Balance approach refers to the degree of congruence between the division of a region into territorial states and national and political identification of the people of the region, as well as to the prevalence of strong or weak states. The two dimensions of this approach are the prevalence of weak or strong states and the extent of congruence between territorial borders and national identities (cf. Miller 2006: 660, 665). Congruence can either exist because of the homogeneity of a nation or because of the prevalence of civic nationalism. Manifestations of internal congruence can be frontier states (if the state is weak) or staus quo states (if the state is strong) (Ibid. 2007: 58, table 2.2). If ethnic nationalism prevails, incompatibility between geopolitical and national borders can cause two types of incongruence: too few states (nations without states) or too many states (states without nations) (Ibid. 2006: 666f). Manifestations of incongruence can be revisionist states and pan-national movements (if the state is strong) or incoherent or failed states (if the state is weak) (Ibid. 2007: 58, table 2.2).

3

4. State to Nation Imbalance on the Irish Island

In the Irish case, one has to distinguish between different phases of the conflict in order to classify its character. During the early phase of the conflict, from the 16th to the 19th century, the Irish state was part of the English Kingdom and later Great Britain and therefore had no right for self-determination. The British state's interest in the conflict was minimal, if not inexistent, although it caused the conflict with its settlement policy. During this time it was probably a rather cultural conflict, coinciding with religious believes, a clash between the English way of life including settled down agriculture and Protestantism and the Irish/Gaelic way of life including pastoralism and Catholicism. Only in the early 20th century it started to become a primarily political conflict, a conflict about borders, the possibility of partition, and territorial integrity versus national affiliation, combined with social and cultural aspects (Kuusisto-Arponen 2001: 121). When the two Irish states were created in 1919 and 1920, they both were weak states because they both remained part of Great Britain. After the Republic of Ireland had gained independence in 1922, it tried to reach agreements with the UK to keep at least some sort of control or claim over Northern Ireland, like it did in 1985 with the Anglo-Irish Agreement, in which the UK recognised the Republic's right to be consulted in issues concerning Northern Ireland (Mulholland 2002: 145). Ireland never gave up on its claim on Northern Ireland to be a part of the Republic which made it an irredentist state because it always hoped to annex the six counties of Northern Ireland. Once the state became stronger, it could be considered to be a revisionist state because it still hopes for reunification: The pursuit of unification, which was formalized in the Anglo-Irish Agreement, is codified in Article 2 and Article 3 of the Irish Constitution (Leach/Williams 1999: 875; Verfassungen Irlands 2009).

Northern Ireland in contrast was an incoherent state during the hot phases of the conflict. Part of Great Britain and therefore not autonomous, it was extremely weak and not able to control the paramilitary forces' criminal and violent activities for centuries (Mulholland 2002: 74-107). Even the British soldiers that were deployed to Northern Ireland in order to restore law and order were not able to change the situation, their presence rather led to a spiralling of violence because of their extremely violent behaviour against often unarmed demonstrators (Aoláin 2000: 15). The state became stronger after the Good Friday Agreement in 1998 so it could now be considered a status quo state, since it wants to remain part of Great Britain.

The United Kingdom's jurisdiction and policy concerning the conflict can be divided into three phases: the militarization phase from 1969 until 1974 during which soldiers were deployed to Northern Ireland, being tasked with both civilian responsibilities and restoration of order. During that phase, their extensive use of violence and the introduction of emergency powers led to an escalation of the conflict. The conflict then was prolonged during the following 'normalization' phase from 1975 until 1980. The UK tried to demilitarize the conflict parties by handing back control from the military to local law-enforcers; an attempt that failed and led to the third phase from 1981 until 1994, the counter-insurgency phase (cf. Ibid.: 15). The UK tried only half-heartedly to end the conflict and to reach a peaceful resolution. This left the two weak Irish states more or less on their own what in return allowed the violence to continue and the conflict to remain unresolved. Only later on, in the 1990s after the ceasefire the UK put more effort into a peaceful solution to the conflict, probably because the Irish Republican Army (IRA) had started to also attack places in England, especially London, in the late 1980s (Mulholland 2002: 159). Once the UK and the Republic of Ireland became members of the European Community (EC) in 1973 one must also take into account the EC's, and later the European Union's (EU) influence on this conflict. This issue is discussed briefly in the next chapter of the paper.

With regards to the State to Nation imbalance on the Irish island, one has once again to distinguish, this time between the two points of view, the loyalist and the republican. As mentioned before, the partition of the island did not only create two states but also two minorities, the island-wide Protestant minority and the Catholic minority within Northern Ireland (Bollens 2000: 190). Therefore, there are two different ways to look at the situation. From a republican point of view, the State to Nation imbalance manifests itself in a too many states outcome: The majority of the Irish island is Catholic; therefore, the island should be one unified Irish state, independent from Great Britain and with one Dáil Éireann (the Republic of Ireland's Parliament) for all of Ireland in Dublin. From a loyalist point of view on the other hand there are too few states: They consider themselves British, not Irish, and therefore part of Great Britain, not part of Ireland. Although one could argue that the loyalists have realised their aim because they have their own state which is part of the UK that is not the way they see it. For the loyalists, there is always the fear of reunification, especially because of the Irish Republic's claim on their state. This is why they do not only support the existing political structures of

Northern Ireland but also see the maintenance of those structures as an active political goal they have to fight for and defend against competing alternatives, especially against republicanism (cf. Leach/Williams 1999: 875f).

5. The Impact of the EU on the Conflict

Thomas Diez *et al* developed a theory about EU influence on different border conflicts: border conflicts within the EU, for which they chose Northern Ireland, border conflicts at the outer borders of the EU, and border conflicts closely related to the EU. They argue that EU influence on conflicts can be direct or indirect and the extent to which the EU can exercise influence depends on the conflict. There is also the possibility of a negative outcome (cf. Diez *et al* 2006: 563f). The authors also define four stages of conflict, depending on the degree of securitization, that means the degree to which one conflict party defines the 'other' as a threat, and the extent of infiltration of social life by this securitization: The weakest being 'Conflict Episode', followed by 'Issue Conflict' and 'Identity Conflict', and 'Subordination Conflict' being the last and most intense stage of conflict (cf. Ibid.: 568).

The Northern Ireland conflict is categorized as a conflict of subordination, transforming into an identity conflict after the Good Friday Agreement. Diez *et al* reason that the Agreement well succeeded in limiting widespread intercommunal violence, but that it also reinforced the articulation of contradicting unionist and republican identities and that therefore, the conflict is deadlocked at the stage of identity conflict (Ibid.: 569).

The four pathways of the EU's impact to transform border conflict defined in the article are related to two dimensions: whether the impact is created by direct, concrete EU measures or the indirect effect of the integration process and whether the impact is visible in concrete policies or it has wider social implications. Concrete, actor-driven measures aiming at policy change have a compulsory impact and consist of incentives for conflict actors to change their behaviour, such as for example offering membership. Concrete, actor-driven measures aiming at the society have a connective impact and consist of support for cross-border and cross-communal projects. The enabling impact is created by the integration process and alters policies by relying on a specific actor within the conflict parties to link its political agenda to the EU. The EU legal and normative framework allows this actor to justify actions or opinions that might otherwise have been considered illegitimate. The constructive impact is also created by the integration process but alters social life because it 'aims' at changing underlying identity-scripts of the conflict and supports the construction of identities that sustain peaceful relations between the conflict parties (cf. Ibid.: 572-4).

Although both the UK and the Republic of Ireland are members of the EU since 1973, the compulsory impact has been limited. This is because the EC differed extremely from the EU: It did not provide any facilitating conditions for a conflict solution because back then, border conflicts were considered a domestic problem andfell under national jurisdiction (cf. Diez *et al* 2006: 576).

The connective impact instead is widely acknowledged: The Interreg Program and the PEACE Program, both financial support programs for cross-border and cross-communal projects, were very successful and led to an immense desecuritization of intercommunal relations, especially along the border between the two Irish states (Ibid.: 582).

Also the enabling impact had a considerable effect in Northern Ireland, especially during the 1990's when the republican Social Democratic and Labour Party (SDLP) succeeded in linking its conflict resolution agenda with issues of European integration. However, there was also a setback when the nationalistic Sinn Féin, the political arm of the IRA, emerged as the largest Catholic party after the Good Friday Agreement. Moreover, there was a "lack of popular identification with the SDLP's pro-European ideology and with the EU in general" (Ibid.: 578). But the EC/EU also offered an opportunity and legitimacy for the British and Irish heads of state to meet on a regular basis, something that would otherwise had been met with greater controversy (Ibid.: 579).

There has been almost no constructive impact in Northern Ireland. But integration did offer an alternative frame for identity construction and made cooperation with the other side possible, something that was impossible before the Good Friday Agreement (Ibid.: 585).

6. Conclusion

The Northern Ireland conflict perfectly demonstrates how conflicting identities can create a conflict and how the weakness of the involved states can prolong it. If the UK had had a greater interest in a solution, it would have probably not lasted for centuries. The prevalence of ethnic instead of civic nationalism facilitated the emergence of an imbalance and consequently the emergence of a long lasting conflict.

The fact that finally a peace agreement could be reached was due to the conflict parties' wish for an end to the violence and also due to the influence of the EU. The EU and its normative and legal framework not only provided the British and Irish heads of state with an 'excuse' to meet regularly, but also with an 'excuse' for controversial policies and decisions. The "[…] enabling impact of the EU has played a major role in conflict transformation, either through a long-term socialization of policymakers into European normative discourses […] or the empowerment of alternative desecuritization discourses […]" (Diez *et al* 2006: 587-8).

It is very important to bear in mind that this conflict is not completely solved and that it is no longer about religion. It is about the clash between nations and the clash between their contradicting interests, about territorial integrity versus national affiliation. The problem in this conflict is the incompatibility of the interests of both conflict parties, because "[...] each group's best hope for the future is the other's worst fear" (Leach/Williams, 1999: 876).

7. Bibliography

Aoláin, Fionnuala Ní: The Politics of Force – Conflict Management and State Violence in Northern Ireland, Belfast: The Blackstaff Press Limited, 2000.

Bollens, Scott A.: On Narrow Ground – Urban Policy and Ethnic Conflict in Jerusalem and Belfast, New York: State University of New York Press, 2000.

Diez, Thomas, Stephan Stetter and Mathias Albert: The European Union and Border Conflicts: The Transformative Power of Integration, in: International Organiza tion, 60(3), 2006, pp.563-593.

Kuusisto-Arponen, Anna-Kaisa: The End of Violence and Introduction of 'Real' Politics: Tensions in Peaceful Northern Ireland, in: Geografiska Annaler. Series B, Human Geography, 83(3), 2001, pp.121-130.

Leach, Colin Wayne and Wendy R. Williams: Group Identity and Conflicting Expectations of the Future in Northern Ireland, in: Political Psychology, 20(4), 1999, pp.875-896.

Miller, Benjamin: Balance of Power or the State-to-Nation Balance - Explaining Middle East War-Propensity, in: Security Studies, 15(4), 2006, pp.658–705.

Miller, Benjamin: States, Nations and Great Powers: The Sources of Regional War and Peace, Cambridge: Cambridge University Press, 2007.

Mulholland, Marc: The Longest War – Northern Ireland's Troubled History, Oxford: Oxford University Press, 2002.

Verfassungen Irlands: Verfassung Irlands vom 1. Juli 1937, 2009, http://www.verfassungen.eu/irl/ (rev.: 15 January 2011)